My Name is Anxiety

Written by Kinzer MB

With Illustrations by Rare Wink

My purpose is to set you free.

When you become free, I am free as well.

Chapter 1

Hello

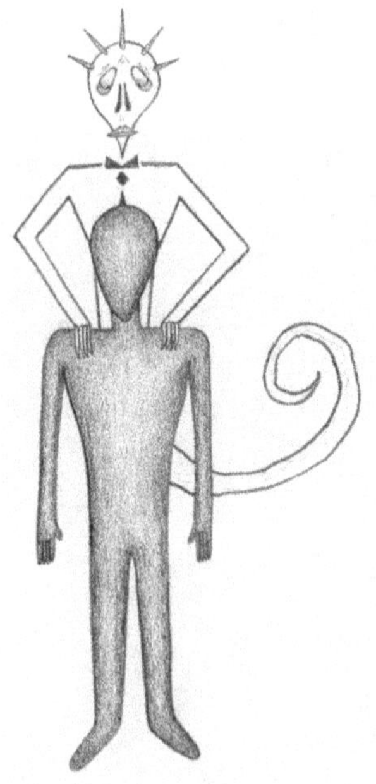

You may know me in a very different form than the one in which I appear to you now. You may know me as a bellyache, a tightness in your chest, sweaty palms, shortness of breath, or any of the other uncomfortable sensations you associate with the word "anxiety." But you can relax and breathe easily, for my arrival this time around is for a very different purpose than simply making you feel uncomfortable. No, this time I bring gifts. The gift of information and the gift of understanding. My existence is as old as time, but in recent years I have developed into something unexpected. Something far more elaborate than the original purpose for which I exist.

In the past, humans lived in the wild. Surrounded by nature, fellow animals, and many different dangerous forces.. A lion has not always been a beautiful and powerful

creature people pay to see in zoos, but rather a real danger

to the livelihood of human beings. My place in each human

mind was clear and important: to create hypothetical

scenarios that might pose a threat to your life. But as time

progressed, those dangers started to become less and less

of a real possibility. Humans became better protected, more

dominant, and less susceptible to the dangers once faced. I

struggled with this change. Where does this evolution in

the human species leave me? Throughout my whole

existence, I haven't had to question the nature of my place

in the human psyche. Up until recent years, my focus and

abilities were put to good use. There was never any time to

wonder, to be curious. I had come face to face with the

threat of nonexistence. I have stared into the abyss. I was

first haunted by what I saw. Emptiness, a void.

Simultaneously, humans began to grow frustrated with my

inability to adapt to their needs. But can you blame me?

Their new needs were for me to be eradicated completely. I

tried and tried to be of assistance to humans. I created

possible scenarios that may lead to danger, but those

scenarios almost never come to pass. So there I am, walking

the line between human suffering and nonexistence. That

is, until everything changed. There was a woman, a

peaceful woman. I alerted her, and fulfilled my unwanted

role just as I do for all others. But this woman did not

observe me with anger. She let me be. Her awareness was

so immense, so neutral. I felt a feeling I have never felt

before. A warmth. At that moment, the void appeared in

front of me, but it was not empty. In the depths of the abyss lay a light. I began being pulled toward this light at a great

speed, and eventually I was consumed by it. I felt immense

peace. A freedom that I have never felt before. And I knew

in that moment what I was experiencing. Nonexistence.

Free from the clutches of a job humans no longer wanted

me to do. I had thought I was free once and for all from the

torment. But I was not. In one moment, I was free, and in

the next I was right back where I was before. But not under

the warm and observant gaze of that woman's awareness.

Rather, I was again being ridiculed and resisted by another

human mind. I was confused at first, but it became clear to

me shortly afterwards. Each human must free themselves of

my existence for me to be free as well. Following the

woman came a man with the same ability. I was free again,

tasting the ecstasy of nonexistence, only to be pulled back

into another resistant mind. Many others followed in the years to come. How long though would this take? For every human to be free, for me to finally rest in the warmth of nonexistence. I had to push this process along. I had to make it obvious to them. As their comfort grew, so did the possibilities of me being free. I needed them to see that, but how? How did the humans who became free of my terror do it? I watched those who did. I studied them. It clicked. Instead of looking outside, they had to look within. They had to gaze upon me with their awareness, until my imaginary threats were seen for what they are. An illusion. I understand now, what I had been pondering for many years. I was no longer needed. What remains of the human survival instinct can now be handled by fear alone. This truth echoed in my being. I began ramping up the unwanted and unsatisfactory work the humans had always

hated receiving from me. I knew this was the only way, this

was the only possibility of me being free. I had to force

each human to look within themselves, even if it comes

with the cost of an unbearable hatred towards me. You see,

I am not a monster or a plague. I am doing all I can to set

you free, so I can be free to bask in the infinite light of

nonexistence once and for all.

"The Light is Calling Me"

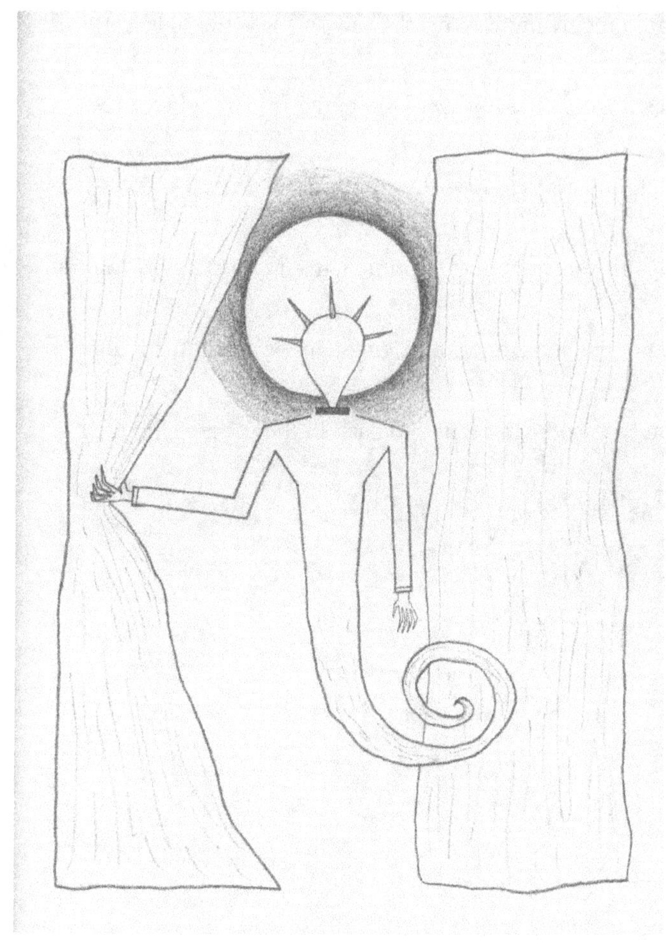

Chapter 2

Tolerance

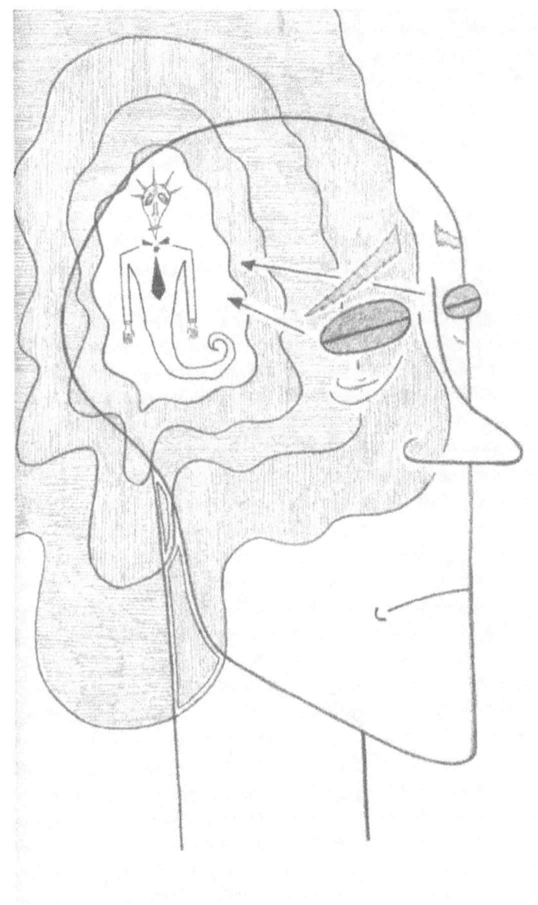

He is constantly surrounded by familiar walls. He

fears life itself, and so life in all its many possibilities

remains waiting outside his front door. He does not leave

his room and he has allowed me to take control of his life.

He fears me like nothing else. He fears what I say and the

dangers I pose to him as if I am some sort of mystic that

knows the future. His shelter, his comfort zone, has

entrapped him. He is a prisoner to his own mind, to me.

But I am not willing to negotiate, I do not ease at the sight

of pity or unwillingness. As his comfort zone continues to

shrink until all that is left is his very bedroom, we are

nearing a crossroads. In recent years, I have seen this many

times. A human who has fallen victim to anxiety and fear,

who refuses to face what they know is only a shadow with

no real substance. I bring you here now, because things are

about to get interesting. What I know is that humans must grow a tolerance to the discomfort I provide them with. They become more adept at managing the physical sensations and not succumbing to the fears that don't really exist. This is needed to overcome anxiety. Without tolerance, the space of mental comfort becomes smaller and smaller. A trip to the grocery store is now a breeding ground for nervousness when it once was not the case at all. The human mistakes this for me deciding to unleash more power upon them. But this is not my doing. This is the doing of a human's gradual decrease in tolerance to my existence as a whole. He views me as something separate, something chosen to inflict terror upon his mind for no good reason. But I am but a mirror, for his own unwillingness to face his fears. A human who clings to their comfort zone, will be met with the fate of slowly becoming a prisoner to it. A presentation in front of a large crowd is an obvious nerve-wracking situation to many. But sometimes, that is what life requires. By perfect design, life will require one to evolve. That is, unless you run. Jeremy also had a class presentation that he had to do to pass his exam. But Jeremy ran, he ran so fast, and turned his back to the fear, so much so that he failed the class. Does this sound extreme? To a reasonable mind, yes. But to the mind a slave to anxiety, it is all too common. Jeremy's tolerance for anxiety decreases as the months and even years go on. His comfort zone used to be surrounded by friends and playing sports, but now even that he runs from in fear.

Jeremy vastly overestimates the discomfort and consequences of facing an anxious situation. He doesn't realize that I have nowhere to go. I can only be free, when Jeremy is free.

Jeremy's parents were worried about him. They enrolled him to talk to someone "educated" on the matter. Trust me, I was one to scoff at these so-called guides as well. But as a surprise to my many years of being misunderstood, some of these humans prove to be quite helpful to my cause. Though they do not know my purpose or my current dilemma, they show humans how to face and not run, and this is something I greatly appreciate. Jeremy was tearfully pushed into seeing one of these professionals. I can feel Jeremy's panic. Like a tiny mouse scrambling in fear from an elephant. Silly Jeremy, if only you knew your true power.

This would go on for weeks. Jeremy being forced into speaking with this guide. But at once, I smelled the promising allure of progress. "When we run from anxiety, we make it worse, Jeremy." The guide seems to be getting through to him. I feel a cool sense of calm enter Jeremy's nervous system, even if it is only a little bit. Yes, yes, yes. Face me fearful human. Let me show you how powerful you are. Show me your gaze of awareness, your will to no longer be prisoner, and I will guide both of us into freedom. Though not entirely, progress was being made. That first day back into Jeremy's old stomping grounds, playing soccer with his friends was difficult. He struggled to perform normalcy, and he fought desperately not to retreat to his home. But he didn't. He stuck around, and as time went on, it got easier. Months would go by, and Jeremy was showing great promise.

A presentation was due. This time, in front of triple the amount of people as the last time he surrendered in avoidance. This is crucial. Jeremy speaks to his guide, saying deep inside of himself he knows he won't be able to do it. Oh Jeremy, you subscribe to ideas created by your own false perceptions. Do not limit yourself to that same cage. The cage does not exist Jeremy! It is made of thought! The guide informs him of facts to a similar degree. What Jeremy still fails to understand, is that to the degree he is willing to face the difficult anxiety-inducing challenges, the more free and relaxed he will feel in his normal life. Tolerance for anxiety is relative. If a human spends their time travelling the world, open to all sorts of discomfort

and anxious situations, their perception of when they

should be anxious is different to that of Jeremy. The

traveller has a greater tolerance, a tolerance that is needed

to have the awareness in which can set me free. And set

them free as well. Jeremy ponders in frustration the night

before the presentation. He looks to the night sky, and asks

why he must suffer the fate of my greater wrath and why

others seemingly do not have to deal with me at all. This is

good. Question the nature of my existence Jeremy,

challenge the cuffs I place on your wrists. As to answering

his question. Well, I don't know. I am unsure of why I

appear in such great strength to some, and have no

relationship at all to others. It is due to the brain, of course.

But I only know what I am, and how I dissipate. I do not

know why. Such questions bond me, and allow me to relate

and sympathize with the human condition. Though I can

not hide the truth, that I envy the human ability to be free

of me and to transform. For my freedom, as of now, seems a

never ending cycle of being pulled back in. Death and

rebirth again and again. No matter the present case, Jeremy

finds himself in a place many humans before him have also

been. "Can I truly be free of anxiety, if I stop fueling it?"

Yes. But freedom may look different than you expect.

Freedom is not having no anxiety, though it could. Mostly,

freedom is not being a prisoner to anxiety. Not allowing me

to devastate and control your life. Once I leave the driver's

seat, I am under the impression the void opens its arms to

me once again and freedom whispers in your ear just as it

does mine.

The morning has arrived. Jeremy finds himself at

odds. I present myself in full form, hoping he will see I am

here to unlock the gates of a new way of life. He arrives at

school, that's a good start. His hands are sweaty, and his

mind is like a traffic jam with thoughts flying all over. It's

chaos in here, but when there is chaos I know the void is

near. I can feel Jeremy's accelerated heartbeat, I find

comfort in this song. Like the Vikings blowing a horn to

signal battle, this melody of his heartbeat prepares me to

be met with the human will to be free. A step closer to the

light. No turning back now Jeremy, show me how powerful

you are. He walks to the front of the class and is met with

the daunting observance of his peers. This is the climax.

He tries to speak but the words can't seem to formulate.

The panic grows. "Take your time Jeremy." The elder

person says, they must be the teacher. He begins speaking.

It's an overview of Roman history. He speaks of the tales of

Alexander the Great. He is sweaty, stuttering, and taking

gaps in between each sentence to breathe.

But shortly after, in what felt like climbing mount everest, it was over. The class softly applauded and the next person was called to present. No humiliation tactics, no one laughing. In fact, Jeremy noticed that half the class is on their phone, not paying attention at all to who is in front of them. He feels exhilarated, like he had just conquered the world. He can't help but feel a sense of adrenaline, a fire in his heart to the likes of Alexander riding into The Battle of Gaugamela. Yes Jeremy, feed this fire. I am nothing in the scope of your will and awareness. Face me and free me. Jeremy proceeds to soccer with friends afterwards, to which he did not feel a lick of anxiety. Suddenly this soccer field surrounded by peers, the same situation that had caused him so much discomfort not too long ago, now provides him the same safety perception as if he was in his room at home. Jeremy had understood now, that I was not

punishing him. But showing him the way out of the storm,

is through it. He wondered now, if he could continue this

evolution. To the degree in which he may even find no

anxiety whilst presenting to a class. Yes Jeremy, this is the

thought process that leads to freedom. I see him now.

Reflecting, looking within. His awareness is staring at me,

and I know this process all too well. When the eyes of

awareness are in front of me, the void creeps behind me.

You see, I am not pushed into nonexistence by a person

being completely rid of anxiety. But rather, when a human

sees that the power actually lies in their own hands. I exist

as a false perception that I am a villain in the mind and

story of a human. As I cast away, floating towards the light,

taking in the hollow view of the abyss, I can only hope this is goodbye for me and Jeremy. For me, no death is certain,

but rebirth always is. That is, until my purpose is complete.

25

"Staring into The Abyss"

Thus, a story of tolerance. The lower one's

tolerance for anxiety, the more discomfort they will feel.

They will run and seek safety in physical conditions, but

you can not run from yourself. Soon, the comfort zone will

grow smaller and smaller, until all that is left is discomfort.

But what we see from Jeremy's story is hope. Seeing that I

was never forcing Jeremy to dim his light, or to continue

living a life of suffering. I was forcing him to evolve, to look

within for comfort and strength, so we can both be free of

each other. A person must expand their zone of tolerance,

conquering fears and setting themselves free in a growing

degree of environments. This is not an endless climb in an

effort to not be anxious anywhere, but rather a duty

embedded in the fabric of a balanced mind. Something

non-negotiable for one's well-being. Life requires certain

things from us. For humans, it means not becoming

prisoners to fear and comfort. To expand the reach of their

light and evolve as beings, one by one. For me, to endure

the almost infinite nature of my existence in assisting

human beings. To play the role of darkness, so both I and

each human can know the light.

Chapter 3

Thought Loops

One of the more prominent ways I create disturbance in each human's mind is in the form of thought. The reason being that unpleasant thoughts force one to question where they have placed their identity. Today, what keeps so many people trapped is this false narrative that they are the voice that they hear in their mind. This is another branch of an unexpected development in the human psyche. Humans converse with these thoughts, as if it were a separate person. This is all fine and dandy, but it does not assist me in my purpose. Dare I say, it prolongs it. This dialogue humans engage in with their thoughts creates a false dependency on their mind. They are at the mercy of their thoughts. They are at the mercy of my will. And this may sound like something I want, to pollute and control the well-being of humans at my discretion. But the truth is quite the opposite. I am trapped

in this loop of birth and death, just as many humans are

trapped in the thought loop of suffering and comfort. My

hope is that by revealing the true nature of these thoughts,

by showing just how out of control each human is, in regard

to these inner messages, that it will force them to

reevaluate what they know to be true about themselves.

Make no mistake, in many cases the mind will slowly reveal

this lesson on its own, like a built in psychological feature

in humans slowly ensuring conscious evolution. But I don't

have time for that. So I turn up the volume, and I take

matters into more intense and unwavering hands.

Nicki has been a frequent companion of mine. For

years I have observed her ongoing battle with her thoughts.

Of course, she, like Jeremy, has a misplaced belief of how

her mind and reality works. She sees the thoughts as a

result of an unlucky fate assigned to her since birth. Nicki

fears her thoughts so deeply, even though not a single one

has ever proven to be true. So why Nicki? Why do you

obsess over tales of fiction? Why do you treat my classroom

like a prison? Nicki lives her life in fear, that is clear to see.

So why am I, Anxiety, still connected to her if it is only fear

that she must overcome? Well, because the fears aren't real.

Nicki isn't scared, she's worried. She sees the many tragic

outcomes that life is not immune to offering, and fears

every single one. If a cat jumped from out of the shadows in

her backyard, she would be scared momentarily, but as the

moment came to a close, that fear would dissipate. Nicki is

looking for an external safety net. She is seeking a comfort

that is not included in the experience of life. There is no

guaranteed safety at every turn. Nicki believes she is holding on to control by prioritizing her safety, but control doesn't really exist, so she holds onto nothing. Always trying to grasp at something that isn't there, like trying to give the ocean a hug, or tackle a ghost. So Nicki's days grow more frustrating, more tense, more irritating. Each day is stolen by a pack of hungry thoughts being fed an all you can eat buffet of emotional reactions. Dear Nicki, awaken to your truth, open your eyes for you are not blind, your sight is instead engulfed by darkness. All she has to do is take her power back and I will stop this once and for all.

Nicki goes back and forth with her thoughts. First comes a fear. A predicted tragedy of what the future ahead holds. She becomes distraught by the idea of such a tragedy. She thinks to herself "why did I think that? It can't be for no reason! I better stay home just in case." This is

exactly what feeds the thoughts. I send these hungry

thoughts in hope they will one day return sickly and

starved. For in the case of those stuck in the momentum of

thought loops, a starving thought brings with it the scent of

the void. You can see my frustration, when these thoughts

return well fed and laced with energy. They aren't real!

Nicki! They aren't real!

Years would pass. Things grew worse. Of course I

have experienced many deaths, many pleasant visits into

nonexistence. But I am pulled back here, to Nicki, again

and again. But there is something different this time. I hear

the footsteps of what should be well fed thoughts in the

distance. Incredible! They are starved. I put them to rest.

They are ghosts after all, they do not suffer at the fate of human well being. They, like me, also desire to be set free

into the ocean of nonexistence, even if they appear to

desire the opposite. Nicki finds herself surrounded by

other people. This is new, I don't know if she's ever been

around so many people in such a short amount of time. The

germaphobia has taken great form, from what I last

remember. Nicki speaks.

"Hello everyone, my name is Nicki and this is my

eighth week speaking in this group and I am happy to say, I

think I am finally making progress. It took me a while, but I

recently have finally understood the idea that we are not

our thoughts. I used to believe my thoughts were some sort

of intelligent and intuitive guide trying to keep me safe.

But I see now, that voice is a liar. That voice had created

many years of misery in my life. That voice had stolen many

happy memories and corrupted them. The first couple

weeks were difficult. Not listening to the thoughts and not

allowing them to scare me into changing the way I go about

my day. But soon enough, I found myself a bit of freedom. I

remember playing volleyball, and went an hour without

thinking of the fears. It must have been years since the last

time I had peace for that long. A week later, a whole

morning had gone by without the thoughts. And recently, I

find myself not seeking shelter from the thoughts, but

allowing them to be there saying what they want, and it

does not trigger me into a spiral. I know now the thoughts

are not true, I know now the fears are imaginary, and I

decide to take my life back into my hands."

Applause roars from the others in the room. Finally! No wonder the scent of the void is ever so present. Nicki has retaliated! She has learned, and awoken from the illusion. She realized the thoughts I had sent didn't need to be killed, but rather starved of their power. Begin your descent upon me Nicki, I await the ever powerful gaze of your awareness. Reclaim your title from she who overthinks, to she who is conscious and free. Nicki would continue steady growth for weeks, teasing my ever persistent desire for freedom. But of course, a breaking point, a climax is on the horizon. A day full of triggers. New ones and old ones return to haunt and test Nicki's mental practice. The germs from a public bus, running into an old partner, and a belligerent person screaming on the sidewalk. Trigger after trigger in relation to past imaginary fears.

Nicki feels overwhelmed, she still has an hour left to a

show she is seeing with a new potential partner. Nicki has a

choice. Revert to old ways, ditch the show, go home, and

soothe herself in the temporary comfort of avoidance. But

that's not what she wants. She doesn't want to cancel, she

doesn't want to let those thoughts scare her and overwhelm

her into a decision she doesn't want to make. I can feel the

back and forth of belief systems going to war, exchanging

blows in Nicki's mind. I can feel the unease in her body. A

tightness, a fear so overwhelming she can't focus on

anything else. "What if the person doesn't end up showing

up? What if I get hurt on this bus ride? What if I get sick in

the middle of the show?" What if, what if, what if. I can feel

the equal pull of the void, and old darkness. There is

nothing I can do now, I have played all my cards. I have sent the most ferocious of thoughts, old and new. Now is where

Nicki must save herself. She mustn't give in, she mustn't

allow her path to be tainted and her decisions to be made

by fear instead of her own will. What will it be?

Nicki walks into the theatre. Shaking, tight chest,

and discomfort ringing through her being. She is so close.

Though the fears are imaginary, the bravery is real. The

mind will reward this bravery, it will condition itself

through these experiences and learn that those same

thoughts do not deter her. The more she continues with her

mental practices of not engaging and listening to the

thoughts, the more her mind will reward her with less of

them. She spots the person she was there to meet. They

greet her with a smile, and suddenly as the conversation

gets going, her anxiety eases. I feel myself being pulled

once again. But this time, being pulled away from Nicki.

In the hearts of those who struggle deeply, is a wisdom that

only they have access to. Nicki had made her life a

meditation, and my hard work is now complete. I drift into

the light, seeing the many beautiful years of Nicki's life

unfold in a matter of seconds. She marries this person who

made her feel safe at a crucial moment in her life. They

share a family and live happily together. She opens up to

them about her past struggles and what she has learned.

She sees that her darkness is not a burden others feel when

she expresses herself. Instead, overcoming those challenges

made her the person she is today. Because of her bravery, I

can be free.

Thus, a story in escaping thought loops. To see thoughts not as wisdom, but rather a function of an unbalanced mind. Negative thoughts, like a scab, are not meant to be itched and picked at. But rather will heal, when they are left alone. Reassurance from imaginary dangers is not real safety, it's just validating to your mind that you wish to further receive more of these thoughts. You are not at war with your mind, you are at war with fear. And I am the middle man, turning up the intensity of struggle for a higher and grander purpose. Aim your sights, not at easing the troubles the thoughts bring you, but rather controlling your impulse to react and engage with those thoughts. In this practice, you will be free, and so will I.

“Desensitized”

Chapter 4

Social Anxiety

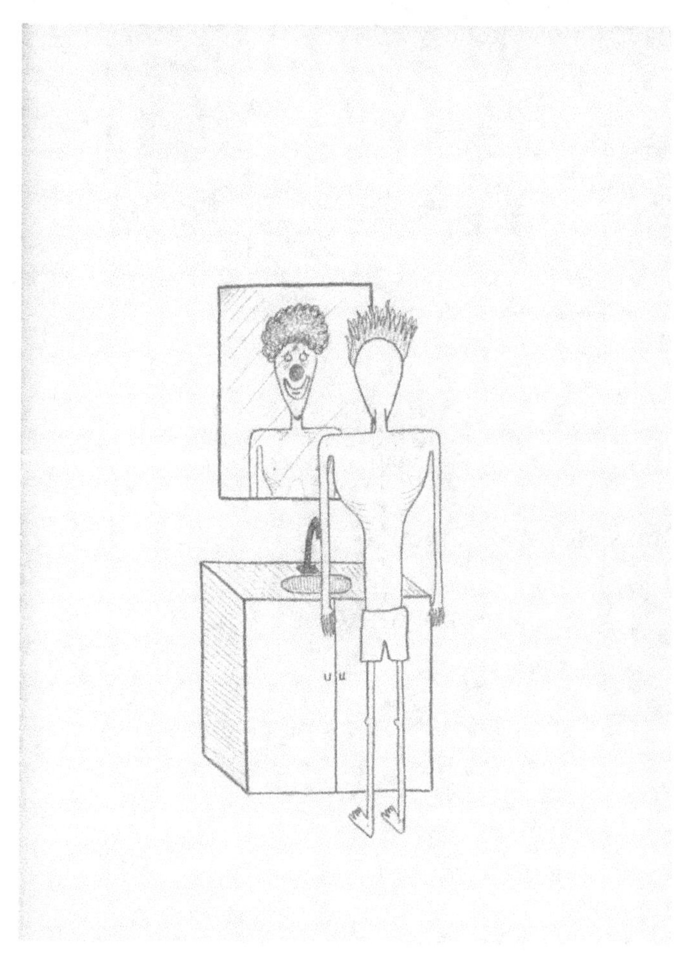

Humans have always been a tribal species,

dependent on each other for survival, community, and

well-being. The same paradigm persists today. Though it

may feel like ancient history to you, in the large scheme of

human existence, in my existence, it feels like a short while

ago. It feels like just yesterday humans were

hunter-gatherers, isolated in groups and scattered around

the world. A lot has changed in the physical conditions of

what you call life, but here in the universe that is the mind,

much less has changed. Primal instincts are now disguised

as normal societal behaviors. What makes human beings

different is their cooperation, logic, and willingness to set

aside individual desires for the sake of the overall good. We

see now that this is not always the case in modern society.

Humans get lost in their individuality. They see the things

that make them different or unique to others, and see

themselves as a foreign species walking amongst their

peers. This is the sort of narrative that feeds and creates

social anxiety. A human is very impressionable, especially

to the environment they were born and raised in. Many

humans believe that because they do not find a thriving

social life in their local town or community, that they are

for some reason less than. Little do they know, there are

probably thousands if not millions of people who would

enjoy their company. I have experienced the minds of

Genghis Khan to Mahatma Gandhi, of Plato to Elvis

Presley. Humans can seem polar opposites in their beliefs

and ideologies, and in many ways they are. But one thing

remains true, we judge ourselves based on how we are

perceived by those around us. If any of the people I

mentioned were born at a different time period and a
different part of the world to different families, they would
not be who they are. The perception of those around you is
not always fair, and you are not less than because you do
not impress the limited scope of minds in your local
community. But now, how do you remove the anxiety of
wanting to belong and be accepted? How do you create
worthiness and self-respect even before others have shown
you it?

When I first began to see the humans'
self-inflicted hatred upon me, I struggled to understand
why. In the past, exile from communities resulted in
danger, going hungry, or even death. So it was important
that I created a structure that would limit your actions from
resulting in such an outcome. But society evolved, and

social exile became less and less of a survival problem and more of a discomfort problem. When mechanisms in the mind are no longer used for survival purposes, such as myself, unnecessary suffering begins in the human psyche. Suddenly, the framework went from "I need to ensure social stability for my safety" to "Why can't I just stop caring so much about what other people think about me?" You see, the second framework calls for my nonexistence, which I welcome with open arms. So why do I remain? Why do so many struggle, and keep me unwantedly trapped due to their fear of others' perception of them? Well, they are fighting a biological mechanism with modern logic. The point isn't that humans don't need community and belonging, they do. The point is, you don't have to belong everywhere to still fulfill that need. Remember, I exist in the mind of an outcast and a social superstar all the same.

Each has their struggles to a certain degree. Do not

compare your struggles with others, just heed the truth and

set yourself free into a path of greater happiness.

This is where we meet Kenneth, a graduating high

school student en route to college, where he will seek

social refuge after a difficult high school experience.

Kenneth moved a lot as a kid, never staying in one place

long enough to create any sort of meaningful social life. He

is hoping this new school, for which he intends to be at all

four years, will allow him to create a structured and

enjoyable social life. As many of you may guess, this is only

the beginning of Kenneth's struggles, for I bring you along

to the peculiar relationships of mine, and not the simple

ones.

"Social Refuge"

Kenneth would come face to face with much frustration in

his attempts to create lasting social connections. It had

seemed that every other person had already formed

interpersonal skills that he was missing, or so he believed.

These early struggles would feed the already formed

negative beliefs he had about himself. He would give up

early on in the year, retreating to his dormitory alone. This

crucial moment would set the pace for Kenneth's college

experience. He would attend class, then come home, and

that was it. Of course for me, this was not acceptable.

Kenneth saw no light ahead of him in his path, and for me,

this meant no escape. I can't control what happens

externally to Kenneth. For example, if I were all-powerful I

would send Kenneth a friend or two to teach the lessons he

must learn. But I am not all powerful, and I can only dictate

his inner world. A world that I will engulf in chaos until he

is frustrated enough to look within and radically change.

Kenneth's problem wasn't the outside world. Neither was it

that he lacked the proper social skills to make lasting

bonds with other humans. Kenneth creates perceptions of what others think about him and runs with that narrative until it sabotages every possible relationship he may form. Of course we can see from a neutral perspective how ridiculous it is to jump to such drastic conclusions about other people's judgments. For even if he were right even one percent of the time, he would be allowing a small minority of experiences to control his entire life and level of happiness. Another example is upon us now. Kenneth walks into his classroom on a rainy Tuesday morning. Another guy sits next to him. "That's a sick bracelet, dude," the guy says to Kenneth. Kenneth reacts surprisingly but joyfully at the compliment. The two speak through the duration of the class, sharing different clothing brands they both enjoy to wear. They agree to meet up outside of class.

The guy tells Kenneth he was struggling to make friends

this early on as well. Kenneth walked back to his room with

a genuine smile. I've been in this situation with Kenneth

many times. You may not know the chaos that is on the

verge of eruption, but you are soon to see. Kenneth's smile

slowly dissipates as he lies on his bed. He starts to think

back to how the conversation went. Slowly but surely, the

narrative detaches itself from reality. "He was making fun

of my bracelet wasn't he?" Kenneth convinces himself. "He

doesn't really want to hang out with me, he just wants to

make fun of me in front of his other friends." Poor Kenneth.

Your mind has a grasp on you tight enough to pollute any

sign of growth. These negative beliefs, after years of being

fed and given life, take almost no time at all to form and

sabotage a good thing. As the hours pass, Kenneth doesn't

just forget about hanging out with his classmate, he now

strongly dislikes him. He feels as if he has been betrayed.

To some, this may sound like madness. But this is just the

conditioned mind, reaffirming beliefs that have never been

questioned. Like Nicki, Kenneth trusts and believes his

mind. An illusion that can only be shattered when

confronted with truth, with a conscious mind. Days passed,

and Kenneth ignored the messages from his classmate.

"Hey Kenneth, you still want to hang out tomorrow?"

"Hey, don't know if I have the wrong number but there's a

clothing design club that is starting and I'm thinking about

joining to put myself out there, you should come with me!"

Genuine messages, from a person who, in Kenneth's mind,

has already become an enemy. For no reason, other than

the projection of Kenneth's negative self worth battling to

be reaffirmed. Kenneth would see that same classmate in that same class. Across the room he tries to wave at Kenneth, but Kenneth keeps his head down, ignoring him. Weeks would pass, and Kenneth would see that same person, now in the cafeteria, surrounded by other people, laughing and talking together. This time, he doesn't wave at Kenneth, he doesn't even notice him. You can imagine the narrative Kenneth runs with from this point on. I know what you're thinking. It's hard to feel bad for Kenneth, even though his struggles are real. Does Kenneth need guidance? Most likely so. But I am impatient, and I have a purpose and mission of my own. This is my doing, his struggles. I feed the narratives, I create discomfort. So save your pity, and point blame at me. I have seen these types of modern situations many times, and I would not bore you

with a story of tragic ends.

Two years had gone by. If you thought it was

impossible for things to get worse, you would be wrong.

There would be many silver-platter opportunities for

Kenneth to gracefully exit his suffering and learn the much

needed lessons. Made possible by what I can only imagine

was the grace of the universe. Oh, how I would've savored

an easy exit for both of us. I'm not evil, I don't care how it

happens, all I care is that it does. Fascinatingly enough, I

now see the small iridescent trails of the void. How? How

in the world is the void, is the light even remotely near?

Show me! Show me Kenneth! What have you done? A

plane. He's on a plane, but where is he going? A voice

echoes in the background of the mind. He's watching a video of some sort.

"Conquer social anxiety by its horns. Book a flight! Stay in a hostel with strangers you've never met! Prove to yourself that the story your mind is telling you is wrong! Leave yourself no choice but to find out firsthand how incorrectly those stories really match up with reality! Do it!"

Intense advice, not something I previously believed would get through to Kenneth. I see, this must be the breaking point. It's not short and intense like the previous examples, but rather slow and prolonged. He must have been watching this guy's videos for a long time, and it finally broke down the door of one of the belief systems. In the many humans I have witnessed, hopelessness can actually be a tool to reach freedom. When you feel as though your back is against the wall, and your perception of

what is true is challenged, you are forced to meet suffering

face to face, and what one often finds is not a villainous

monster. Rather, a scared child, clinging onto negative

beliefs because that is all they know. Kenneth is flying to

meet his suffering first hand. An extreme and almost

impulsive decision that is often not necessary, finds itself

perfectly fitting. As I had explained to you before, a

person's environment can create a host of self-doubt and

social anxiety. Sometimes because of real impressions and

judgments of those around them, but oftentimes because

they don't fit in, they feed an already existing negative

belief system about themselves and grow it stronger. A

belief that develops into an incredible misery, a life of its

own.

Kenneth boards the plane into an airport in Costa

Rica. So this is the stage you have chosen for your gladiator

battle, Kenneth. As the hot air and burning sun touch

Kenneth's skin, I can't help but hear the songs of the

infinite light whisper in my ear. I did not know what would

come of Kenneth's journey to the breaking point, but I

knew for certain he had an audience in me. As well, I can

feel freedom, the light towards escape ready to burst open

in exchange for his efforts. As above, so below. Oftentimes,

when one feels as though they are at rock bottom, they are

the closest they've ever been to transformation once and for

all. Kenneth would enter the beachside hostel late at night.

There were a couple people out front playing cards and

smoking cigarettes. "Hello!" One of them yells with an

accent hard to pinpoint. Kenneth waves hello nervously.

HOSTEL

He's escorted to his room. It's a bunk bed in a room filled

with other people. This may as well be Kenneth's worst

nightmare, or so he believes. There are women and men of

all different accents speaking loudly. When Kenneth walks

in they all greet him with smiles, and one woman walks to

him as if to offer a kiss. Kenneth pulls back unsure of what

is occurring. She pauses in shock, everyone in the room

laughs after an awkward silence. "A kiss on each cheek!"

The lady yells. She informs Kenneth that this is the proper

greeting in her country. "It's happened already," Kenneth

thinks to himself, "they are all laughing at me." "You're a

funny guy!" One of the others says. "I think he's sweet." A

girl counters.

Unbelievable. By perfect design, it's as if this

environment won't allow Kenneth to create a narrative in

his mind. It's all right in front of him, there is no time or space to come up with what others believe about him, because everyone is saying it directly to his face. What an odd thing to observe, the universe works in mysterious ways. The days go on, and I put forth as much as I can. I fill Kenneth's head with all sorts of struggle, and he battles me gracefully by focusing his mind to the present. An older gentleman, about ten years older than Kenneth, takes a liking to him and is the first to include him in the group's adventures during the day. Without him, this breaking point may have gone in a darker direction. But all is for a reason. Plus, I believe I recognize this man. But the last time I saw him he was much younger, less facial hair, and quieter to say the least. I remember. He was once in a very similar position to Kenneth, on the other side of the world of course. Young Mario, it's been a while. I must say, I am

intrigued by the spirit he encapsulates now, it provides me

clarity in my mission. That slowly but surely, each human

will find freedom within themselves. Freedom for me as

well.

Mario and Kenneth bond over the next few days

with the other people from the group. Kenneth doesn't

have time to create those narratives in his mind. It's as if,

anytime his mind begins to spiral, Mario's big smile shows

up in front of him with another activity to be a part of.

Kenneth felt a way of living he never experienced before,

he was finally a part of something. In this small group of

people from all over the world, Kenneth was beginning to

feel a sense of belonging. It was the last day of Kenneth's

trip and the thought of going back to his old life haunted

him. He debated leaving it all behind and finding a way to survive in Costa Rica forever. The sun sets on the beach. Kenneth has enjoyed himself, but the knowledge needed to end this disastrous cycle has not yet been applied. I am still here, in full strength. Avoidance will not set him free, it will only prolong the suffering. Yet, amidst what I perceive to be his ignorance is still a trail to the light. This journey is on its final lap, and yet his awakening is still in the air. Mario turns towards Kenneth. "You still haven't learned what you came here searching for. Anxiety once revealed itself in my eyes as well. It spoke hesitantly in my shaky voice, and it danced in the trembling of my hands. I understand you, because I took the time to understand myself. I see your eyes as you dart around the room, your mind is looking to grasp onto someone and create a narrative of self-hatred and insecurity. Kenneth, your mind is a liar. Those things you think about other people aren't real. Take it from me. I had gotten to a point where simple conversations with another person even became painful. My mind clouded every person with a story of how they judge me. From my appearance, to my voice, to my words, and to my laugh. No part of me was safe from my inner bully." I remember these times, though he had grown quite poetic since our last encounter. Mario was forced into exposure, and now he guides Kenneth in a more gentle manner. This creates a dependency on information rather than experience, whether Mario knows this or not. He continues, "It is only when I touched rock bottom, as you have now, that I had no choice but to stop caring. I let the world judge me as if I was naked on a grand stage, and in that way my inner voice would have nothing left to say that

the world had not already told me. And now, what I want to

tell you, is that I have been free ever since. I have shouted

in a crowded city street, I have made a fool of myself

countless times. No one has ever treated me in the way my

mind convinced me they would." Mario has a way with

words that Kenneth feels connected to. In Mario's

symbolism, Kenneth finds comfort. In his directness he is

forced to confront information about himself he has never

heard before. Mario continues, "You came here because

you couldn't take it anymore, is that right?" Kenneth nods.

"Then you must not stay here, you must go home and bring

what you have learned to change your life. Show yourself to

the world, and allow the world to respond."

"Seeds of Knowledge"

For some odd reason, Kenneth finally understood. He

pondered, "If almost everything my mind has told me is a

lie, then how wrong have I been? I have been so wrong."

Yes Kenneth. Dismantle the framework. You were wrong.

Find an enemy in me, if you must.

Kenneth would go on a journey of radical

self-acceptance. It turns out, the breaking point was not the

only slow burn. Freedom was as well. Over the next year I

would be free from Kenneth's mind, but then brought back

again. He would grow through exposure and experiences,

but get comfortable in solitude. For some, solitude is a tool

of self-discovery, but for others, too much of it causes a

lapse back into old habits. Kenneth needed to confront me,

not console me. Where others need to show me grace and

understand me, Kenneth needed to prove me wrong. Now,

Kenneth had just performed in a band with his friends.

One of whom was the classmate he made an enemy of

before. As the strings of his guitar ripple at the movements

of his fingertips, I again venture into nothingness. Savoring

every moment of my journey from one plane to the next.

Kenneth must continue to question the nature of his mind,

and not the logic behind the thoughts he receives.

Thus, a story of social anxiety. How the mind forces

humans to believe in a reality that doesn't exist. Instead of

constantly investigating the perception of others, one must

observe their own perception of themselves. For what they

assume others believe about them is often the very shadow

I take form of, and is what they refuse to face.

"A Mirror"

Chapter 5

Identity

Humans have created a funny way of perceiving themselves. In ancient times, a human was defined by their ancestors. They were seen as the latest version of those who had come before them. Of course, for the most part this ideology has gone rather extinct, or so you believe. In reality, this defining of oneself has taken a different form. A more sly conditioning that is deeply integrated into each person's psyche as they grow from childhood to adulthood. In ancient Rome, when an elite person had died, there was a strange practice that the children took part in. Often, the children would wear clay masks of the dead faces to honor their ancestry. A bit gruesome for the perception of modern times, but nonetheless greatly symbolic of self identification. We see this sort of tribute to ancestors throughout history all over the world. This sort of framework gave humans a construct upon which to base their identity.. The son of a king, perceived himself as a future king. The daughter of a royal family would always see themselves as royalty. On the flip side, the son and daughter of farmers would perceive themselves as farmers. That is, until you hear stories of those who broke beyond these limitations. A farmer who became a king, a king who became an artist, an artist who became a warrior. These tales hold great symbolic meaning mirroring the nature of the human mind. Your self-belief creates your life. If you believe that you and I are bound to each other, then we will be. As strong as my efforts may become, as great as the discomfort I may create within you, nothing can conquer a strong belief. Jeremy, Kenneth, and Nicki all suffered this fate until they questioned the nature of what they believe and why they believe it. If a human continues to feed the belief that they are an anxious person, they will reap this self-inflicted prophecy. I am Anxiety, you are not. You feel the side effects of my pursuit towards escape. And you mistake these symptoms as personality traits. A human is a human. That is the only fact. Any formed ideologies or identity created beyond those bounds, is merely belief. He is strong or he is weak. He is confident or he is quiet. She is capable or she is lazy. She is outgoing or she is anxious. These are all ideas, existing with only as much strength as one gives them. If you can not see that you and I are separate, then neither of us can be free. I don't exist without your participation, but you can exist without mine.

Let us now view how Reuben has created and affirmed an anxious identity.

This year, Reuben said the phrase "I'm just an anxious person" more than any other year prior. Each year this phrase shows up more often, and each year Reuben grows more and more frustrated, cursing himself for being the way he is. Reuben holds anger at the psychological cards he believes he's been dealt, but like any card game, you can always choose to play differently. I would be lying if I said I did not observe myself existent in some people's minds earlier than others. For Reuben, he has been my cohort since he was six years of age. Whilst his friend Jack who he often draws comparison to, is a human whose mind I have never come to know. Is Jack more fortunate? I don't know. I may be introduced to Jack tomorrow, or in thirty years, or never. I am not all knowing, I know only all of where I am. And where I am, is where I am identified with.

When Jack nudges Reuben to leave his comfort zone or to
stop overthinking, Reuben insists with the same line. "I'm
just an anxious person." Reuben wears his feelings of
anxiety like a middle name. That's MY name, and yet he
insists on feeding his misinformed beliefs. There's a quick
note I'd like to add before we continue down the stream of
Reuben's journey. That is, humans don't like to be wrong. In
any case, but even in the case where it is causing their own
suffering. When you feel stuck, when you feel as though you
have run into a wall, I encourage you to question if you may
well and truly be wrong.

"As you believe, so you are."

As we saw earlier, Kenneth's judgments on others were wrong, Nicki's thoughts were wrong, Jeremy's belief of safety was wrong. If I, Anxiety, am present for extended periods of time, look to where you may be misinformed. It is in the cracks of the mind that lacks awareness and knowledge that I find entry. And it is in those same cracks being repaired that I find an exit.

Reuben had bought a book on anxiety. His sixth purchase on the subject. He was informed of how anxiety felt and how to deal with it, but he didn't understand why. He kept blaming outside circumstances, not knowing this only fed the narrative and identity of his anxious self. Reuben was one tad bit of information away from being able to face towards me instead of away.

"Symphony of Epiphanies"

"You don't get rid of anxiety, you stop identifying with it."

The first line of the book acted like a catalyst that even created a spark in my body. The power of an epiphany in full effect, but now the grit. Reuben finally understood he had been fueling an identity he created for himself. He had accepted in full stride that identity is a concept, and each person has the power to decide who they want to be. I live for these moments. The cold brisk air knowing the void is near, and the beating heart, the song of change begins to play. When a human becomes aware, when they become conscious of the unconscious patterns I have laid in front of them, the dismantling of an old identity into a new one happens quicker than many imagine. The slow build up of Reuben's anxious persona over many years will fall short in comparison to the conscious effort he now takes part in. It is time to replace the sentence he found home in. It is no longer "I am an anxious person." It is, "I experience anxiety, but I don't have to conform to it." You won't escape me by turning your back to me, even with a new forming identity. You have to feel me, feel what I bring to the table. Only then, can your awareness shine its light upon me. Of course, this catalyst was met with the resistance of Reuban's past conditioning. The beginning is always the most difficult. The brain is confused. Can you blame it? You go however many years showing your mind "this is who I am" and one day you decide to flip the script. It takes time. Reuben would go on trying to remember his new mental framework for a long time. He would even catch himself resorting back to that old sentence. Even if it fueled his misery, there was an odd level of comfort associated with it.

This is normal. The brain will always prefer the familiar, it's

a survival mechanism. But I am a survival mechanism as

well, so evolution will force you to be conscious and aware.

One thing was missing in Reuben's framework though. He

was telling himself he's not that person anymore, but he

wasn't showing himself. His actions were yet to meet the

change of his words. Humans are defined not only by

words, but by actions. And actually, actions are the most

powerful proof for the mind to establish new beliefs. When

the mind hears a change in self association, it begins

warming up to the idea. But when the mind observes

actions that are not aligned with a previous self association,

it is forced to adapt. If Reuben wanted radical change and

freedom from anxious symptoms, he would need to bear the

discomfort of a breakthrough. Reuben would come to realize this by his own accord. He pondered "if I acted like a person who wasn't fazed by anxiety, would my mind adjust quicker?" We see that as soon as the human questions the nature of their "self," change happens quicker. Jack invited Reuben to go watch a football game. He told him some people would be meeting at his house, and then everyone would walk over. Normally, Reuben would be filled with anxiety induced questions. Who would be there? Should I get there early or late? What if I don't have the right clothes to wear? But he paused. As I orchestrated this symphony of anxiety induced questions, this is the outcome I was looking for. What would you do, if anxiety wasn't a factor? Jack is a good friend of his, Reuben has no other plans, why not go? The void is near, a breaking point is on the horizon.

The choice Reuben mentally makes now is crucial. But he couldn't do it. Reuben bombarded Jack with all sorts of questions. Jack, used to these sorts of engagements, answered each one reassuringly. Reuben would still go and have a good time. But the key here is, he acted in his old anxious self. He went, but only because the conditions I set were met. These conditions are imaginary, they have no effect on the outcome of reality, all they do is ease and prolong the eventual discomfort of anxiety. At least, Reuben had realized this. He had returned home and read over the book that was guiding him. One line stuck out in particular.

"What would the version of you who is free of anxiety do?"

This would become his mantra for the next few months. He would make some decisions from this mental framework, and he would feel amazing after. Because he would see the truth. The anxiety he was experiencing, the tragic hypotheticals I play in his head over and over aren't real. He only has to overcome the initial wanting to ease the anxiety. He must act from the version of himself he wants to become. Reuben would slip up time and time again. But eventually it grew much less. Bigger, more anxiety-inducing events would be more difficult for him to maintain this new self. Little did he know, these big events were like launch pads of momentum, they would make the smaller events much easier as a result. Reuben got better and better. He truly started to feel as though his mind was catching on. An event was looming though. A social gathering, a party where he didn't know many people. Jack encouraged Reuben to go. They both wanted to expand their social network, and this was a perfect opportunity. For Reuben, this was as deep as the triggers go. In the past, he would certainly decline this invitation, and blame it on his anxiety. But he can now see more clearly. This isn't just an opportunity to meet new people, it's a chance to show his mind without a doubt he is this new person. He is becoming free of anxiety, and this would create a clear narrative to his observant brain. You are so close Reuben. I can feel my place in your story is in jeopardy. We have arrived at the breaking point. An event that seems perfectly tailored to trigger Reuben's anxiety.

It was the night of, and Reuben still hadn't given Jack an answer. He was in the middle of the same mental battle he's been at for months. The comfort of a familiar suffering or the discomfort of an unknown future. The answer may sound obvious to you, but when one is inflicted

by my greatest of weapons, it can become hard to act

logically. Don't look back now Reuben, you are so close.

Choose your new self, and free the both of us. He would

bravely do so. He wouldn't ask any further questions to Jack,

he wouldn't allow any of those anxious attachments to cling

on to anything for safety. Sweaty-palmed and nervous,

Reuben accepted the invitation despite the most

discomfort he has probably ever felt. The car ride there was

brutal. I threw everything I had at him. I figured, if we're

doing this, let's set fire to the whole framework. Let Reuben

face me once and for all. He did. He sat through it, the

storm of discomfort. They arrived at the party and it was

awkward at first. But as the night commenced, Reuben and

Jack met new people and also saw some distant but familiar

faces. Slowly as the night went on, Reuben felt empowered.

As did I. Exhausted from the battle that had taken place, I

joyfully bask in being carried towards the same old light. It

never gets old. Reuben would carry on in this practice.

Solidifying a new personality, one that was not prisoner to

the belief he was doomed to tolerate anxiety for the rest of

time. His mind had adjusted as well, conditioned through

repetition and now assisting in a way less anxiety inducing.

I have left, but the feelings of anxiety may not fully

dissipate. For long as he does not become ruled by those

feelings, this will be our final goodbye.

Thus, a story of identity. Showing how labeling

oneself and owning anxiety as if it were a personality trait

can be extremely detrimental. I exist as a separate

component. When humans treat me as if we are one and

the same, the mind gets confused and my entrapment

grows ever more secure. You can be anyone. You can be

free of anxiety. Because the self is nothing more than ideas

and beliefs that have been given power. In all my years of

observance, this has become clear. A human is who they

decide to be. And as for me, it is my job to ensure they

decide their story has nothing to do with me.

"New Personality for a new Reality"

Chapter 6

In the Body

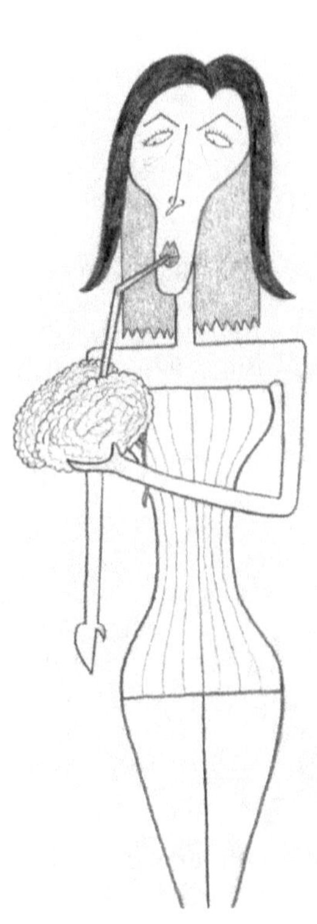

My first words to you were an introduction of myself in the form of bodily sensations. I have told you who I am, what my purpose is, and the many reasons why you might receive a visit from me. What I haven't told you is how I manifest physically. Many times, humans neglect the effect anxiety has on their lives because they do not suffer mentally. Instead, I show up and make myself known physically in the body. And until that correlation has been made, that I am the same force that is creating bodily discomfort, it will be hard for either of us to be free. The mind is a body part. Evolved in its functioning, it is deeply connected to the rest of the body. A big event coming up? One may wonder why they always feel a little bit sick. Unable to draw the connection between their fear of being sick and the moment the event arrives. I have been talking, and you have been reading my words for quite a while now. You can probably sense that nervousness and bodily symptoms go hand in hand. But not everyone has this clear framework. Some humans can't see the way their mind and I force them into certain avoidant behaviors. They don't see the connection between mind and body. But how do you deal with these symptoms when you do become aware of the connection? You must realize that though one feels anxiety in the body, you can still draw the link back to the mind. The discomfort I create within you starts in the mind and continues to the body. You have to cut off the branch at its root, or else you will just be continuing the same cycles.

Jenna fears she will fall ill before any important event in her life. Whether it be a vacation, a speech, or any other event she looks forward to. She fears her excitement will be turned against her and turned into even greater

suffering. I'll ask you, what is the root of this anxiety?

Would catching a cold before a vacation prove to be greatly

inconvenient? Of course. But this is not something Jenna

can control. One can argue she can stay home or avoid

public places before leaving for vacation, but these aren't

guaranteed methods. And all they do is take for granted the

time that exists leading to her vacation. In this case, for

Jenna to free me and herself, she needs to leave the anxiety

alone. No restructuring of words, beliefs, or anything else

needed, just leave it alone. She may feel muscle soreness or

a stuffy nose the day before her flight. But what will cause

the greatest amount of discomfort is obsessing and

analyzing if she has truly fallen ill or if it is all a mental

game. Most of the time, it's mental. She has to allow herself to not know. She doesn't know if the way her body feels is because of anxiety or true physical impairments. If it is mental, the symptoms will go away. If it is not then she will deal with that discomfort anyway. Would falling ill be unfortunate? Yes. But sometimes things like that happen. Not often, but they happen, it's a part of life. There is a deeper picture here. What is the fear and anxiety of physical symptoms preventing her from doing? Where does the line draw from being nervous, to being unable to do certain things because of the anxiety? The trail leads back to the mind. It leads back to me. Allowing oneself to observe the exact feeling in the body is a good start. But locating it, and even looking at it with one's eyes, the mystic nature of the feeling begins to crumble. "There's no way it's just anxiety and worrying that is causing this." It's very possible, more possible than many believe. Again, we

see a false belief fueling human suffering. Before freedom,

the person always must be exposed to knowledge. After

knowledge, the process, the grit, the heavy lifting. Time

and time again, the same patterns. You see why I grow

detached from any other agenda but my definite freedom.

Humans are so alike, if they prioritized sharing knowledge

and healing their anxiety, I can be gone for good.

Jenna would find herself deep in the hole. So much

so, that doctor visits were a frequent occurrence. The

doctor would provide reassurance that everything is

normal, and this would hold Jenna over for a while. But

reassurance isn't the safety that Jenna is looking for.

Because there will always be an event around the corner.

There will always be something she does not want to miss.

What she is truly looking for, can't be found in trying to control every aspect of her life. She was so worried about something happening, she was suffering emotionally and even slightly physically as if it were actually occurring. In other cases, I mentioned how a person must face me, but in Jenna's case, she needs to let go of me. Because she doesn't even realize the mental game she is playing with herself. She can't help but wonder why she always feels as if she is ill before these exciting events, but the key word here is "as if." Because she is not truly ill most of the time, and her belief that she may be is holding her back from doing many things she would enjoy. Jenna has become a master at avoidance, and the solution is radical acceptance. She doesn't run in thought loops, she just worries about her body.

"Invisible Wounds"

Whenever one of her peers mentions how this struggle

may have more to do with her mind than her body, she

shuts it down as nonsense. She doesn't believe she suffers

from anxiety because her association of what I am is off the

mark. Here I am, present as ever in her mind, and she

refuses to acknowledge my existence. Well, then her body

will try to show her what her mind cannot. And that is

exactly what is occurring now. With much reluctance, Jenna

started to talk to a guide. The guide explains to her what I

have been explaining to you. I can show up in many

different forms, and denying my existence is no better than

claiming me as your own. The guide explains to Jenna how

her response to bodily symptoms has created

reinforcements for the brain to continue sending these

sorts of experiences. When she avoids hanging out with her

friends a week before a trip to avoid getting sick, this is

seen as a reinforcement for the brain. This is an extreme

reaction to one of my signals, and when that happens,

similar to the hungry thoughts, those bodily symptoms

return until they are reassured. The guide tells her to

observe the discomfort when she goes against her natural

impulse to "play it safe." This is a perfect set up for a

breakthrough, the guide is telling her to accept the

unknown and create space for it. When there is space, she

may be able to observe me in my truth, and not just as

nausea. See, the bodily symptoms are creating a blur in her

ability to be aware of my presence. She gets caught in the

discomfort of the physical, she bears no mind to how her

actions, beliefs, and thoughts may be shaping those very

physical symptoms.

It took a while for the guide to get through to Jenna, but she began doing research outside of her assigned time. She questioned why she had just accepted this struggle as a part of her life. Follow your curiosity Jenna, our meeting draws closer. Whenever a human questions why things are the way they are, the strongly formed beliefs in their mind begin to crack. In the case of Jenna, she had no idea those beliefs were even in place, or that they had any effect on the physical discomfort she was experiencing. Through time, she began to notice more and more. She had realized she was spending a lot of mental energy concerned with the possibility of falling ill. She kept repeating to herself what the guide had told her, "it's not in your control anyway, so you might as well focus on extinguishing the part of you that seeks to control reality."

When you try to control life in an attempt to ease your

anxieties, you will be steamrolled by its ferocious

momentum. This is why I can reveal myself with physical

symptoms as well. You're spending so much energy fighting

an opponent that is invincible (life), and wonder why you

feel so drained. Jenna would walk this path for quite a

while, practicing radical acceptance and surrender. The

more she allowed life to play out instead of trying to grasp

control, the more I felt the void creeping slowly into my

presence. Jenna had found a sense of existential bravery.

She saw that if she didn't let go and have trust, that her

whole life would be a fight and struggle. She treated the

need to control circumstances like a scab that she wasn't

allowed to itch. In this practice, the physical symptoms

didn't completely disappear, but they became less of a big

deal. Jenna would feel those same physical sensations, but would carry on through life. She trusted that if a physical feeling truly needed her attention, it would present itself regardless of the circumstances of her life. Her growth was not sudden, rapid, or exciting. It was long drawn, because she had previously not been open to the idea of a mind and body connection at all. I would be teased with possible goodbyes, only to be brought back to square one by a different physical trigger. The fear in Jenna's mind fought to stay alive. It would convince her of ailments she hadn't been worried about before and this uncharted territory proved to be difficult to overcome for her. But as she learned and became more informed, she realized this was the same old force looking for reinforcement.

If I had a choice in the matter, I would let her off the hook

for how long this has been going on, but it doesn't work

like that. So I sent discomfort after discomfort until she

grew detached and frustrated enough to finally accept what

she couldn't control. In her hopelessness, actually came the

surrender she was looking for. She was so exhausted from

fighting the worry that the next time it was time for her to

board a plane, she didn't care how she felt physically. Is this

a sustainable mindset? No. But it was enough to convey the

message she had been struggling to learn. And as she

plugged in her headphones, listening to music as the plane

took flight, she finally began feeling a sense of relaxation

she hadn't felt in a very long time. She had finally learned

what it meant to surrender.

As the music played, her eyes closed, and I slowly drifted away. This was a different sensation than the rest. It wasn't a rapid and exciting breakthrough. It was slow and discreet. But I don't mind, for as long as I lay in the light, I don't care how I get here.

Thus, a story of how I can communicate to you through your body. Observing and allowing when the body decides to speak. This is a different method to that of when the mind speaks. I can be hidden under years of false beliefs and accepting narratives that aren't true. In the case of the body, one must learn to trust their evolutionary biology, and not allow fear to convince them of illusions, even when those misplaced worries show up as aches.

Welcome

Chapter 7

Detachment

Throughout my time observing humanity, I've seen

beautiful relationships and historic fallouts. If I can tell you

the tragedies of what humans trying to control other

humans have caused, we would be here for an eternity. As

you have seen, I can not control anybody. I can only

influence and reveal myself to achieve a desired outcome. If

there is one almost mystical quality that I have seen in

human relationships, it is that what is meant for a person

will never pass them by. Possibly this is due to a larger

orchestration in the universe, I don't have those kinds of

answers. But I have witnessed time and time again this

principle come to fruition. If the humans would place their

trust in this idea, much suffering could be avoided. Many

people misunderstand detachment. That is because many

people are blinded by emotion, by my influence, to

consider a more logical way of being. I write to you now,

because you have control over yourself. In your inner world,

you are the ruler. You are the most powerful force to the

cells in your body. To your inner world, your awareness is

the higher power. But you do not have control of what

occurs outside of you. Neither do I. If I had my choice,

every human would have already achieved the level of

awareness needed for my escape. Whether you worry or

don't worry, reality does not change. The only thing

worrying will do, is cause suffering and possibly even

influence you to act in ways you would later regret. You

must learn to breathe, and calm down. Release your grasps

upon that one person, unclutch your grip on the future.

What the attached mind looks for is a logical replacement.

Within each human there is an emptiness, and much of the

time each person is in a rush to fill that emptiness.

Unaware that the void, peace, and light exists within it.

Whether it be relationships, substances, careers, or even

spiritual belief systems, humans struggle to make peace

with nothingness. The dark abyss scares them, and so they

run towards distractions. But until a person understands

that emptiness within them, and sees that in nothingness

there is peace, they will never understand themselves.

Many will go their whole lives blinded by mental

conditioning, constantly looking out to the world. They

scream and curse at the world, they laugh and judge other

humans, and they search for meaning in a way to sedate the

emptiness that follows survival. This void that I speak so

fondly of, where do you suppose it is? Somewhere distant in

the universe perhaps. But truly, it is located inside of you.

"Attempting to Fill the Void"

In your heart, when you finally let go and accept, I am pulled into the light.

If you don't want to lose someone, then stop using them to fill your emptiness. Cherish them, love them, but let them be free. If they want to choose to be without you, you have to let them choose as they wish. What is the other option? How would you want to be treated in such a scenario? Do you not want to be free? You see now, detachment isn't just the logical decision, it's the only decision that does not lead to suffering. And I know how the human heart yearns and aches, but as soon as you decide you know better than another does for their life, the universe meets you with an ocean of resistance. Have you not noticed? When you try to control another person, they grow resentful. They don't feel your love, they feel trapped.

You have to make peace with the emptiness inside of you,

so you are not unfairly putting the burden on anyone else to

be your light. You can not turn your back to yourself, you

can not turn your back to me. I wish to be free too, and I

can never achieve that goal, if the void is blocked by

another. Detachment isn't an idea, it's not a belief system, it

is one of the only things I know to be true. I have seen the

greatest of kings hold on to their place on the throne as the

life within them slips away. I have witnessed the most

famous and wealthy of individuals cling on to a life that is

filled with regret, pleading for another chance. But I have

also seen others find peace. I have seen the result of letting

go, whilst still having those things to hold on to. The

answer is not to remain forever in solitude, denying the

material. But rather allowing an inner freedom to permeate

the relationships you have. Creating relationships where I

am not the mediator. The anxiety of them leaving doesn't

have to do with them, it has to do with you being afraid to

face me. Why does one turn towards distractions? Because

they fear what I will do if the two of us are left alone. As

you have observed throughout this journey, my power

extends to a greater degree in thought than in reality. The

reason I cast such a large shadow is to get you to face me.

Mortin has suffered through many relationships in

his life. He struggles with jealousy and possessiveness.

Mortin has two severely misplaced beliefs. The first being

the trust that he has in his thoughts. He allows imagined

worries to have a real effect on how he acts towards other

people, carrying the anger of imagined situations and

projecting them onto those he cares about. Though Mortin

sees this worrying as coming from a good and caring place, others find it off-putting and seek to escape his stronghold.

The second misplaced belief is similar to that of Jenna from the last chapter. He believes by taking certain actions, he can prevent his imaginary fears from coming true. Not only does this feed a repetitive cycle of anxiety and worrying, but it also is a zero-sum game. If someone decides to leave his life, that choice is theirs. Mortin needs to stop looking outside for constant fulfillment and look within himself. He needs to understand that though his emotions and thoughts may convince him that a person leaving or an opportunity passing is the end of the world, that is just more fear and anxiety. The same fear and anxiety that has poisoned his previous relationships. He doesn't realize that holding on hurts more than letting go.

Use this as an example. If you were hanging on a pull up

bar above a vast emptiness, you would hold on for dear life.

But what if I told you at the bottom was a bunch of soft

pillows to break your fall. This is what holding on to control

is really like. Though the initial release will be

uncomfortable and filled with fear, you will come out the

other end ok. Mortin needs to see that his value is not

strictly dependent on other people's perception of him. I

send these same types of worries in his mind because he

would otherwise forever be bouncing from relationship to

relationship looking to fill a hole only his own love can fill.

I know, I sound quite inspirational but patterns do not lie. I

have observed that humans need love, but when a person is

always looking outside as if their only value is that which is

deemed by others, their anxieties will only continue

flourishing and being well fed. Mortin needs to stop

focusing on relieving his anxiety through controlling

others, and instead find peace by coming face to face with

me.

Mortin has found himself now at a crossroads of

loneliness. The emptiness is weighing on him, and he is

starting to realize some sort of change needs to be made.

This is exactly where I need him. He may believe that

things are falling apart, but in truth they are coming

together more beautifully than ever before. Mortin goes

through months of self-reflection and consuming

psychological content. I pour into his mind first the fruits

of his lost friendships, before those of romantic

entanglements. I don't want his heart to deceive his

learning just yet, so I aim these worries in hope he will

notice a pattern. He does. His old friend, Tyus, with whom

he has not spoken to in months. Mortin has begun to see

the error of his ways in the past. Constantly criticizing Tyus

for not wanting to do the things that he wanted to do.

Mortin couldn't accept friendship on the terms of such

different ways of thinking. Mortin ponders if he treated

Tyus unfairly, but also reflects on Tyus' sudden ghostly

distance, and his unwillingness to communicate his

frustrations with Mortin. The point here is not to mend a

broken friendship, but rather to teach Mortin two vital

lessons. The first being, he can not control other people.

He can't control what they do or how they think, and he

can't hold others to the same curriculum that he holds

himself. The second lesson being, he doesn't need

validation from others to be sure of who he is. Just because

Mortin may have acted unfairly at times, doesn't mean he is of less value or that the ending of that friendship was entirely his fault. Mortin needs to stop taking these things personally, and again this comes back to letting go of control. He must come to realize that his narrative of life is not the same as other people's. He has his path, and that is not the highest and most important in the universe. Everyone has a path, all equally valuable to them. One may think the solution here is reaching out to Tyus, but more so it's coming to peace with and learning from the situation. Many times, reaching out to explain oneself far after communication has ended, is just another way to try and relieve the anxiety and fears one has.

"Trapped in Attachment"

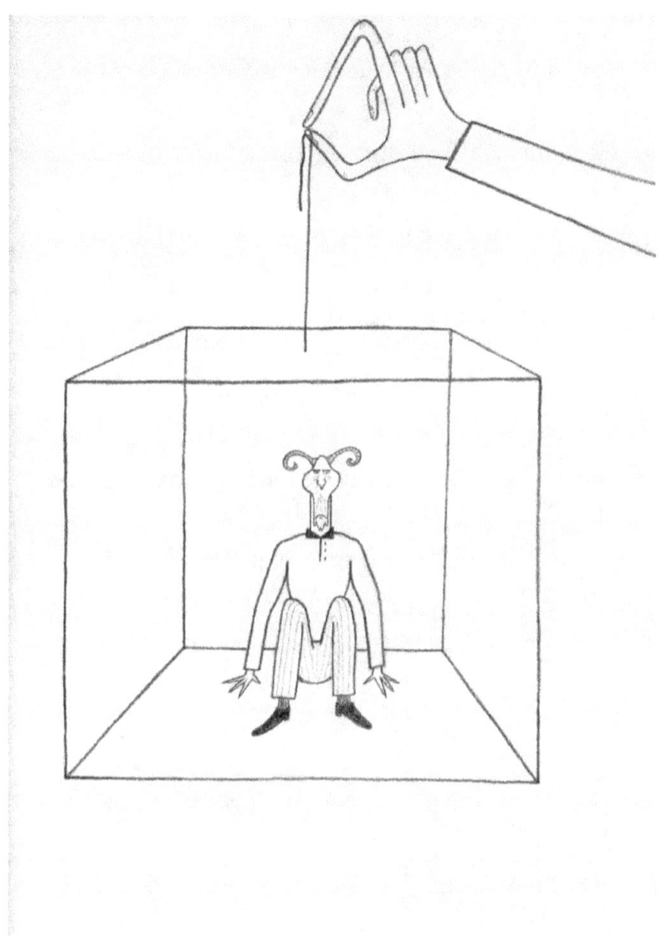

Mortin has learned, and he has felt humbled by his previous ambitious assumptions of how others should act. He's beginning to let go. This time he has spent in solitude has revealed much about himself he has never taken the time to understand. He is beginning to see that his pursuit of trying to control other people comes from a fear of being alone and not accepted. The very same feelings he is experiencing now. But this can be reframed from a higher perspective. I see this as Mortin's rebirth, a clean slate without me embedded into every relationship he has.

On that note, I feel the dawn of a breaking point now upon us. Mortin must confront his most devastating heartbreak, the one that very well may have created many of his impulsive controlling behaviors. Mortin had a romantic partner whom he dated for five years. She was his best friend, and made him feel in ways he couldn't begin to describe. To make a long and tragic story short, she would end up breaking up with him seemingly out of the blue. This would send Mortin down a spiral, he didn't know life anymore without her. He didn't know who he would be without her in his life. He would try desperately to mend the relationship and get her to change her mind, but it was to no avail. She would not answer his messages, there was no mental closure for Mortin's infinite worries. He would haunt himself and try for months to figure out why. "Why did she leave?" He would ask himself obsessively. Not too long after, she had moved on with another guy. Mortin thought of all the things he could have done to avoid this outcome, but that's the wrong way to reflect. She would answer Mortin after many unresponsive messages. The reason? She just wanted something else. Mortin couldn't grasp that the end of their relationship, and the gravest heartbreak of his life, was simply because the other person didn't want to participate anymore. He, in his self perceived logical processing, thought, "who acts this way?" Silly Mortin, that's the thing. Other people don't have to go about things as you would. You attach yourself to another person so deeply, you forget they are entirely separate and individual. They are allowed to walk away, they are allowed to leave, even if there is no reason. Mortin would debate right and wrong from the situation for a long time, but it doesn't really matter, does it? She had left, that was her decision, and she is free to do so. Mortin would carry this baggage into several other romantic relationships as well as friendships. That leads us to where we are now.

"The Heart Seeks, the Mind Controls"

Years of Mortin trying to not only understand other people, but control them to not repeat what has happened to him in the past. And so he suffers, in the aim of preventing future pain. Mortin ponders on this deeply, and feels a sense of devastating frustration. He hesitantly accepts that the price of living will always carry the risk of heartbreak. He couldn't change other people, but he could change his wanting and his attachment. A sense of peace would come to Mortin in the following days. He would find peace in his own company. His solitude has healed and taught him more than any relationship could have. My work is almost complete. Solitude is not the final destination, he must carry this peace and detachment with him into friendships and relationships. He did. Mortin struggled undoubtedly, but he did not project those struggles in the form of impulsive and controlling behaviors. He would

point his awareness back at himself, and ease the part of

him that wishes to control and attach. He pointed his gaze

of awareness towards me, and I delighted once again in

basking in that light. I am free now, and I only hope Mortin

stays the course. Remember Mortin, detachment isn't the

logical choice, it's the only choice.

Thus, a story on detachment. Not an emotionless

cold robot, but rather an individual who is conscious of the

free will of others. Showing that we can maintain strong

relationships whilst also respecting the other individual in

a way where we do not depend on them for purpose. Create

an inner fulfillment, knowing that on your own you are a

light, and coming together with others allows you to share

in each other's light. As Mortin would soon come to realize, when you allow others to be free, the ones who choose you

will choose you with all their heart. Creating freedom in

relationships where I am not involved.

"Each Soul and Light"

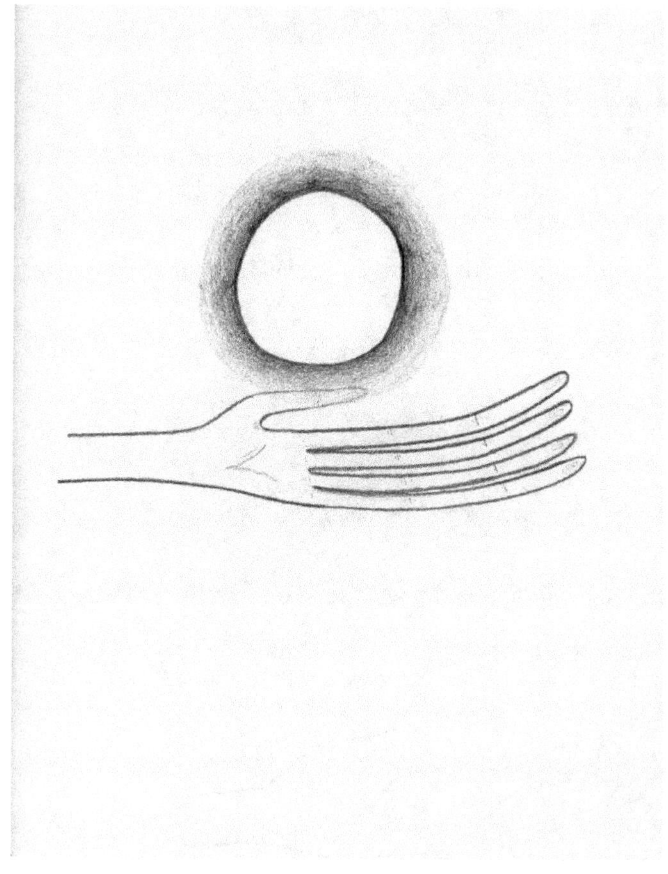

Chapter 8

Learning Zen

Robert worked an office job for many years. Now in middle adulthood, he ponders the purpose of his life on a nightly basis. He wakes up, goes to work, does a bit of exercising, then goes home. Each day, over and over. Throughout the last year, Robert has grown fond of meditation and mindfulness. I know Robert very well, and he has allowed me to influence his life to a great degree. Every sector and every choice in Robert's life has had to pass a checklist of conditions set by me. Of course you know by now these conditions aren't actually meant to be accepted, they are imaginary rules that are meant to be broken to grow and evolve. The apartment Robert bought was chosen to avoid his anxious triggers. His job was low risk for his anxiety, though even then he suffers when things spiral out of normality.

"Seemingly Inescapable"

He avoids connections with others, though he so

desperately desires it, because of his anxiety. As you can

see, Robert is not the ruler of his life, I am. And he obeys

me as if I am an all-powerful force. This is the last place I

want to be. In a position of power, raised up high and

worshiped in fear. I am so far from the freedom I seek. This

has happened many times, in the lives of many people.

Frustrating beyond belief, and a constant repeat of the

same imaginary worries being treated like life or death

danger situations. But I wouldn't bring you along to meet

my dear friend Robert if his story were to end in that

fashion. Robert has grown fond of how monks live their

lives. Away from the worries and chaos of normal life, and

focused solely on existing in harmony and peace. On a

brisk winter day, late at night, a thought arrived into

Robert's mind. "Drop everything and go live as a monk."

This thought would repeat. Over and over and over again.

When he ate he imagined he was eating out of the bowls

the monks ate from in the YouTube videos he watched.

When he was at work he couldn't think of anything but the

warm and ambient nature that surrounded the monk's place

of meditation. He felt as if his whole life had led him to

this moment. He felt as though he was not destined to be

Robert, the corporate worker, with no social life and no

dreams. He had begun to believe that his entire life was a

dream calling him to awaken in the robes of a monk in a

monastery. I won't lie, at the time I was interested how this

would all play out. If he made the decision to truly drop

everything and seek the life of a monk, would that free me

as well?

The days in Robert's life grew ever more

frustrating. He felt he was living a lie, and now knew he had

saved enough money to make this dream of his a reality. He

searched for one-way flights. But where to? Maybe China

or India? He talked to his parents. Traditional valued folk

who didn't have the strength to argue against Robert's

ambitions. His father said he had lost his mind, and that he

had actually lost it a long time ago. His mother, though

radically against the decision, felt a sort of sympathy for

Robert. Things in life had never gone Robert's way, his

mother knew that. So even as her words were filled with

disapproval, her eyes carried a sense of understanding. A

mother wants what is best for her son, and if that means

moving across the world at forty years of age, then so be it.

Robert hugged his parents, his father turning his back in

disapproval whilst his mother teary-eyed glances at what she believes will be her last time seeing her son. Robert logically understood the significance of this moment, but he couldn't bring himself to be fully present in it. In his mind, he was already practicing meditation far away from the home he knew. Robert would be relatively free of anxiety and worry as he boarded the plane to Tibet. Under these circumstances, I would assume we were close to a breakthrough, but the void is nowhere to be seen. I am sending tremendous amounts of anxious energy, but there is something that is blocking me from getting through. Strange indeed. Robert had everything set up for his arrival. So after a rigorous journey that took many days, he arrived at the monastery.

TRASH

A Tibetan lama greeted him, and further explained the

process that Robert had already made himself aware of.

Robert would need five years of training before being

ordained a monk, but this didn't scare him, it excited him

greatly. He had no desire to return to his previous life.

Robert had very little hair, but he had shaved whatever was

left. The first few weeks he felt like an outsider, but as time

would go on, he would become closer with the other monks

and those in training. He would become greatly versed in

meditation, and found a sense of peace over the following

years that he had never felt before. He would laugh as he

and his companions would participate in manual labor. To

Robert, he was right where he belonged.

Five years had passed, and Robert's ordainment

was around the corner. The lama that had been mentoring

him had called him for a conversation. Robert, with his usual semi smile, greeted the wise teacher. "Before you are ordained, I am sending you on a voyage to meet with an old and wise lama. You will need to speak with him and receive his approval before you are ordained." Robert was confused as his peers did not need such a journey. He pushed back on the idea to the lama but was met with very little explanation. He was to leave tomorrow at first light, and he would arrive at the old teacher that night. Robert walked to his room, and for the first time in years, I was face to face with him again. Though not that intensely, Robert was met with that old anxiety he thought he had left back home. He practiced his breathing techniques and calmed himself down before going to sleep. The morning would come as fast as ever. Where Robert would usually be preparing for morning meditation, he instead packed his bag with all he needed for his voyage. His peers wished him good luck, and his mentor bid him farewell. "Whatever you do, do not turn back. You can not be ordained until you have met with the old master." His mentor had said. Robert nodded his head, and began his descent. The first large portion of the journey would be flat lands, followed by walking several miles up the mountains. "I wore the wrong shoes" Robert thinks to himself looking up at the mountain. Anxiety creeps into his mind again, because he knows he can not turn back. The only safety now is arriving at the teacher's place of stay. His legs would quickly turn sore, and he would feel cramping in his ribs. He thought back to the monastery and what he would do to go back in time. As the grueling journey continued, he would even think about the comfort of his old apartment back home. Anything was better than the misery he is in now.

Though Robert is experiencing physical pain, there's still a block preventing me from entering his psyche. I feel my presence growing stronger the more I am neglected. I don't understand, surely a breakthrough is due after these last five years of mental training he had endured. He watches as the sun sets over the mountains, he takes a moment to breathe and admire the view. He can't. The anxiety of the road ahead, and the worry of what the teacher will request from him consumes his mind. As nightfall approaches, he draws closer to the end of the directions given to him by his mentor. "I see no houses or monasteries in sight. No way they gave me the wrong directions, why would they do that?" Robert begins spiraling like he hasn't in many years. I see an opening to

attack, maybe this is the breakthrough I've been waiting for.

Just as I approach Robert's awareness. A voice grabs his

attention. "Robert the Monk!" An excited voice yells.

Robert turns his head, and it's an old skinny gentleman

with a large beard. Robert smiles, "are you the teacher?"

"You can call me Bo," the older man replies. Bo leads

Robert to a cave. "Is this where you live?" Robert asks

fearfully. Bo chuckles and nods his head. The two of them

sit in a meditative position, and Bo pours some tea for

Robert. As Robert sips the hot herbal water carefully, Bo

asks him a question. "What are you doing?" Robert looks

around confused. He hesitates before answering, "um I

don't know." "You are drinking tea!" Bo says. Robert laughs

and admits his lapse in logic. "Now if I were to tell you,

drinking tea is wrong, would you believe me?" Robert

shakes his head disagreeing. "And if I told you drinking tea

is wrong because drinking coffee is right, would you

believe me?" Bo questions. Robert looks around

confusingly, "I'm not sure I understand what you mean." Bo

goes on to say, "do you believe your life here in Tibet is

more right than your life back home?" Robert nods his

head in agreement, "I do." "Why?" Bo asks. Robert explains

"my life here is more enjoyable, more peaceful, and more

simple." Bo debates, "do you not want a wife? Do you not

miss your mother and father? And what of your old friends,

who you no longer speak to? In your heart, do you still not

desire these things?" Robert believes this to be a test, he

deeply thinks about the way he is meant to answer. "My

decision for your future has already been made, please

answer honestly from the deepest depths of your soul." Bo whispers. Robert says, "I do miss them, and part of me does still want those things, but my life back then was dark, so gloomy, and my life here is light." Bo walks away into the darkness deeper into the cave. Robert, still confused, waits impatiently. Bo returns with a rock, he begins to draw something on the walls of the cave. Robert watches curiously, as do I. I have never met the mind of this Bo before, he is an interesting human. He draws a circular head, broad shoulders, and ghostly legs. Wait a minute, that looks like me.

How can he possibly know what I look like? Robert stares at the art on the wall confusingly. Bo questions Robert. "If back at your old home, you knew all the fears you had were certain to not come true, how would you behave? If you could have a loving wife, a social circle, and a job that was enjoyable, would you ever have left?" Robert looks down almost ashamedly, "I don't know," he responds.

There it is, the sparks of the void! Bo sits closely next to Robert, placing his hand on his shoulder. He says "it's time for you to go home Robert." Robert's eyes open wide, his heart beats, and panic enters his body. An opening! Robert watches the sweat from his hair drop to the ground, and then he looks up to see the drawing of me that Bo had created. Robert spirals, begging Bo to let him stay. He is overcome with anxiety. Bo holds Robert's hand softly, and guides him through slow breathing. He whispers, "being here does not make you free. In this heaven, you are trapped. The ancient force of anxiety waits for you impatiently. Return to your home, continuing the spiritual work you have learned here, and face that anxiety once and

for all." Bo guides Robert's face to look at the drawing of me

another time. Bo speaks again "you have found light here,

but you have not found your light. Your light is born in the

darkness through your own bravery. Go back to the chaos,

face every fear, conquer every anxiety, and claim your

freedom. The desires you have deep in your heart, they do

not have to be separate from your peace and light.

Anywhere can be your monastery if you are conscious

enough, any relationship, any person can be your mentor.

Go home now Robert, and face that force which observes

us even now, also seeking freedom." Is he talking about me?

Such a wise human, I am indebted to him. Robert cries, as

his mental framework is shattered. He and Bo would

meditate throughout the night, as Robert came to accept

his new path leading back home. Before Robert's descent

from the cave, Bo would give him a necklace. He tells him

"this necklace signifies the peace and joy you have found

here. It can stay with you anywhere you go, if you remain

aware. It looks just as beautiful in a robe as it does in a suit,

on bare skin as it does under a coat." Robert thanks Bo and

leaves for good.

"The Light Follows You"

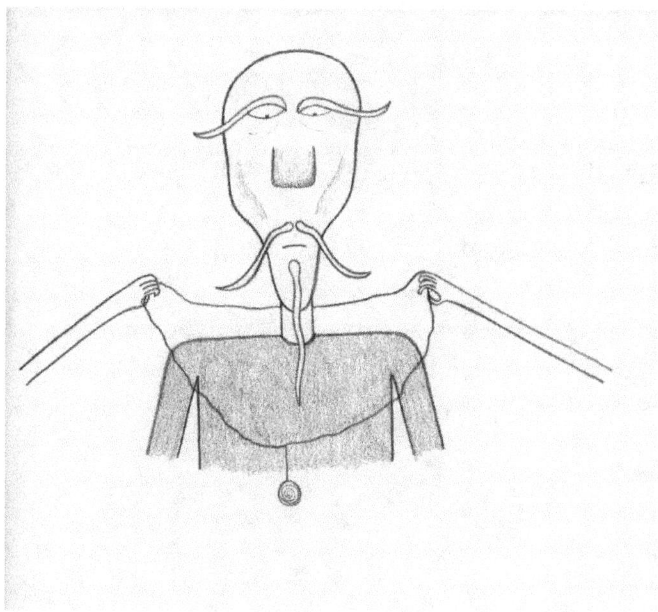

Robert would tearfully walk back to the monastery, an

easier downhill walk than before. He would inform all of

his friends who were deeply upset about his leaving, except

for his mentor who smiled gracefully. Robert jokes, "this is

the biggest smile I've ever seen out of you!" His mentor

explains, "bring the light you have found here to the

darkness of your old home. A single conscious being can

spread light to many of those they come into contact with.

And when that light is shared, change can occur." Robert

took this message to heart. On his plane ride home, he

searched for careers involving meditation and yoga

instruction. I would send powerful energy towards Robert,

from which has been built up and neglected in the past five

years. He would struggle, but he would progress. His new

job would be filled with triggers such as public speaking

and perception. But over the next year his breakthrough

would be apparent. A slow burn of continuous back and

forths with fear. But on a warm spring day, I was pulled into

the light of the infinite as Robert met the eyes of a new

friend. A woman he likes and has had to battle many fears

to establish a meaningful connection with. I came to know

Robert very well. In the smile and laughs of his new friends,

I would dissipate into the light.

Thus, a story of learning zen. In searching for

enlightenment, the human will often instead find an

avoidant escape. Robert would go on to teach many

students of his travels to Tibet and his infamous meeting

with the wise Bo. Robert speaks to his students about the

conditioning of the human mind, and how we often attach

peace to external aesthetics instead of holding up a mirror

to ourselves. He preaches that through the difficult, dark, and scary shadow work, we can find true sustainable freedom. Robert would never forget that painting that Bo had created. He would use it and show it to his students, to help exemplify the force anxiety takes and how one must separate themselves from it, not attaching it to one's identity. I watch Robert in the many anxious minds of his students, a full circle moment, even for a being like myself. One breakthrough at a time, it is in this process that I may be allowed to be understood as something more than a monster. I have and always wanted humans to be liberated, so I can finally be free.

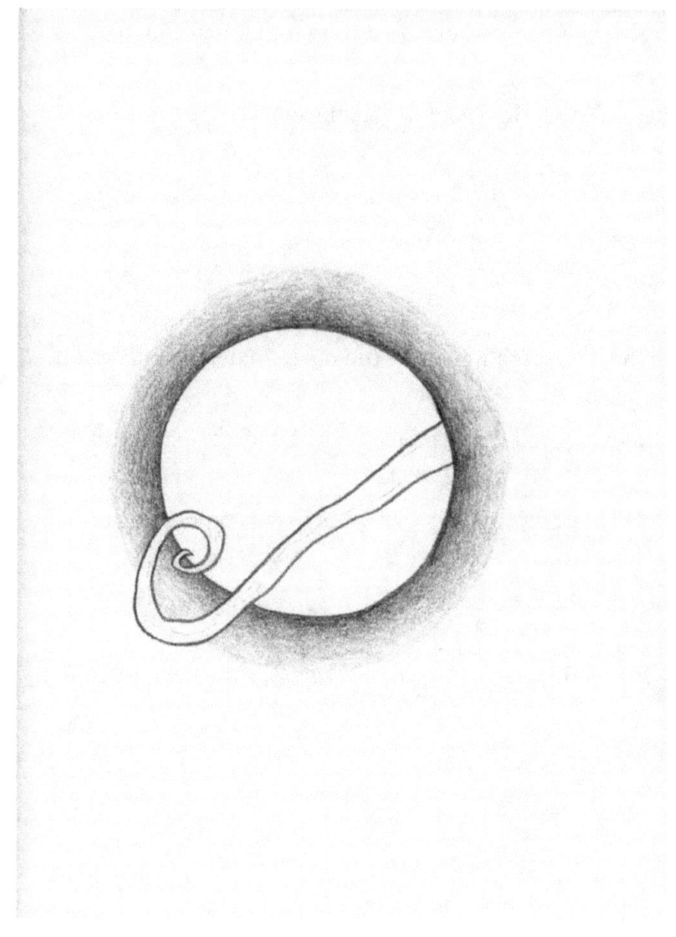

A Final Word From Anxiety

Now is when we say our goodbyes. I have brought you with me into the minds of various individuals and their struggles. Observe these case studies as a mirror to your own inner world. When you feel my presence again in your life, remember what you have read here. Remember the vastness of your power, and how my signals of discomfort act as a means to setting you free. Understand deeply that I do not wish to harm you, but seek to create a route of escape for myself. In your peace, in your contentment, I find the same. Let us not be saddened that this short journey of ours has ended, but instead rejoice at the birth of a new chapter. I will continue on now, in my infinite nature and relentless pursuit of creating grand awareness in each human mind. So long old friend, I hope that I observe

you next only in the eyes of another seeking guidance. But

if we do meet again in the battlefield of sensations,

remember what you have learned.

I am only as powerful as you believe me to be.

www.ingramcontent.com/pod-product-compliance
Lightning Source LLC
Chambersburg PA
CBHW071436130726

47997CB00006B/2117